JAVA

Java Programming for beginners teaching you basic to advanced JAVA programming skills!

Table of Contents

Introduction

Thank you for taking the time to pick up this book on JAVA programming.

This book covers the topic of JAVA Programming, what it is, and what you can do with JAVA programming.

You will learn how to do basic commands in JAVA language, and discover how to begin programming in JAVA.

This book is aimed at beginners who are new to the JAVA language. It serves as a fantastic introduction to programming in general, and will leave the reader confident to step out on their own and begin experimenting with JAVA! It teaches the basics of JAVA, the commands you need to know, and shows you how to get up and running with JAVA.

At the completion of this book you will have a good understanding of how JAVA Programming works and should have a great foundation for becoming a fantastic programmer in JAVA!

Once again, thanks for reading this book, I hope you find it to be helpful!

Chapter 1:
What is JAVA?

JAVA is a programming language designed specifically for use on the internet. It is simpler to use than *C++* language and utilizes a model of programming that is object-oriented. JAVA may be utilized in order to create entire applications that may be distributed among clients and servers in a network or run on a single computer. JAVA can also be used build a small *applet*, or a small application module, to be used as part of a Web page. Applets enable Web users to interact with that particular Web page. JAVA programs can be found in mobile devices, desktops, Blu-ray Discs, servers, and smart cards.

JAVA was originally known as Oak when it was first created. Oak was created by James Gosling in the year 1991. James Gosling worked for a company at the time known as Sun Microsystems and the original purpose for Gosling's programming language was to be used in small electronics such as televisions, toasters, VCRs, and so forth. The purpose of JAVA since its beginning was to be fast, efficient, small, and portable. Sun Microsystems renamed the programming language and introduced JAVA in 1995. After this introduction, the interactive capabilities of the World Wide Web grew exponentially. A JAVA virtual machine is included in all major Web browsers. Likewise, almost every major operating system developer has added JAVA compilers as a part of what they offer in their products. Major operating system developers being companies such as Microsoft and IBM. JAVA is now owned and maintained by a company called Oracle.

The term Java refers generally to a trifecta combination of these things:

- The Java programming language, which is an object-oriented, high level programming language

- The Java platform is a JAVA Virtual Machine that runs Java bytecodes that have been compiled, usually calling on a set of standardized libraries. These libraries include those provided by Enterprise Edition (EE) or Java Standard Edition (SE). Though the JAVA platform and the JVM are designed to work hand in hand, the language itself does not necessarily imply the use of JAVA Virtual Machine, and vice versa.

- The Java Virtual Machine refers to a virtual machine operating at a high performance level, and executes bytecodes on a very specific computing platform. The term 'JAVA Virtual Machine' is often abbreviated and referred to typically as simply JVM.

JAVA vs JavaScript

While both JAVA and JavaScript are programming languages used to develop features or applications on a Web page, it is important that JAVA should not be confused with JavaScript. JavaScript originated at Netscape and is easier to learn than JAVA. JavaScript is also interpreted at a higher level than JAVA, meaning that JavaScript uses a programming language with a strong *abstraction*, or technique for managing the complexity of computer systems, from the details of the computer. JavaScript does lack the speed of JAVA *bytecode* as well as some of the portability, meaning that the running speed of JavaScript is considerably slower than that of JAVA. JAVA applets can run on just about any operating system without necessitating *recompilation* and has no variations or extensions that are unique to an operating system, which makes JAVA generally thought to be the most strategic language in developing Web applications. JavaScript, however, may be useful in extremely small applications that run on the Web server or Web client.

The most recognizable difference between JAVA and JavaScript is the type of applications which they are used to create. JAVA programs are utilized for applications which are either initiated through a Web page or run from a computer's desktop. These programs are standalone programs that usually open a completely separate program window. A computer is not able to run JAVA applications without JAVA being installed. JavaScript is always included in all up to date browsers, however, and will start the JavaScript on a Web page when it is loaded as long as JavaScript has been enabled.

When using JavaScript code, its "thinking" and calculations are always performed on the client side, meaning the computer where the page on the Web is accessed. On the other hand, JAVA programs normally perform all of the main "thinking" and the calculations process within a certain JAVA applet that must first be downloaded or on the server side. Because of the fact that JavaScript runs on the client side, it usually runs faster than JAVA, and is at times even almost instant. Since JAVA programs are run on the client side, it takes just a bit more time in order to process, usually only several seconds or more.

JavaScript uses significantly less memory than JAVA in order to do its processing and also perform correctly. Because of its lower memory requirements and its capability of offering so many varied Web page features, JavaScript is a very common program language utilized in many various pages on the Web presently. JAVA programs, however, may sometimes require that a lot of computer memory be used in order to function properly. This requirement can absolutely cause another program to run at a much slower rate and even cause the computer to slow down altogether. So even while JAVA programs have the innate ability to be developed to do various, often powerful things, because it utilizes a higher memory usage, it can also be a speed disadvantage in some respects.

JAVA Features

The major features of JAVA are:

- JAVA's code is robust. This means that the JAVA objects may contain zero references to other known objects, or data that is external to themselves. In contrast, programs written in C++ and other languages do not have this ability. This process makes sure that the instruction does not contain the address of the stored data in the operating system itself, or that of another application. Either of those occurrences would effectively cause the operating system or the program to *crash*, or terminate. In order to ensure integrity, the *JAVA virtual machine*, or JVM, has a number of checks in place.

- A JAVA applet has other features designed to make it run quickly, in addition to being executed not at the server, but at the client.

- JAVA is much easier to learn than C++, although the language is certainly not learned overnight.

- Programs created in JAVA are *portable* in a network. This means that these programs can be used in other operating systems than the one that created it, without needing to perform a major rework. The source program is compiled into what JAVA refers to as *bytecode*. This bytecode can be run any place in a network on a client or server that has a JAVA virtual machine, or JVM. That JVM then interprets the bytecode to code that will run on the actual computer hardware itself, which means individual computer platform differences, such as the length of instructions for example, can be recognized and dealt with locally, as soon as the program is being executed. Basically, JAVA ensures that it is no longer necessary to produce platform- specific versions of your program.

- JAVA is object oriented. This means that an object can be part of a class of objects as well as inherit code which is common to that class among other features. Rather than the traditional procedural "verbs", objects are thought of in terms of "nouns" that a user is more likely to relate to. A method may be looked upon as one of the object's behaviors or capabilities.

What is Object-oriented Programming, or OOP

Object-oriented programming, or OOP, is a model of programming language organized around data instead of logic, and objects instead of actions. A program, historically, has been viewed as only a logical process that takes input data and processes it, then gives output data. OOP takes the view of object of interest to be manipulated over the logic required to manipulate them. Objects, for example, can range from computer widgets, to a building and its floors, to human beings.

In OOP, the first step is to locate all of the objects the programmer wishes to manipulate, and identify how these objects relate to each other. This process is usually referred to as data modeling. Once you have selected an object to be identified, you would then generalize it. For example, this one particular book would then stand for all books. This generalization defines the kind of data the object contains and any logic sequences that are able to manipulate it. Each separate logic sequence is also known as a method. Objects within OOP communicate with messages, which are well-defined interfaces. The rules and concepts utilized in OOP offer these need-to-know benefits:

- The concept of data class makes possible the definition of subclasses of objects that share all or at least some of the main class characteristics. This property of OOP, called inheritance, reduces development time, ensures more acutely accurate coding, and requires a more thorough data analysis.
- Since the definition of a class is reusable by the program that it is initially created for and also by other object oriented programs, it can be more easily distributed to use in networks.
- The concept of data class allows for a programmer to create any kind of new data that is not already defined within the language in and of itself.

- A class defines only specific data. When that class or object is run the code will not accidentally access other program data. This particular data characteristic of data hiding avoids unintended data corruption and provides greater system security.

What Are Applets

JAVA produces browser run programs which are called applets. Although applets are becoming more and more obsolete as time goes on, they are used to facilitate object intercommunication by Web users and graphical user interface, or GUI.

Before there were JAVA applets available, Web pages and sites were normally not interactive and otherwise static. Such competing products such as Microsoft Silverlight and Adobe Flash have made JAVA much less popular, since it once dominated the market. JAVA runs its applets on an internet browser using JAVA Virtual Machine (JVM). JVM then translates the specific JAVA bytecode into what is known as native processor instructions, also known as native code. This translation allows for indirect platform program or indirect Operating System (OS) execution. JAVA Virtual Machine supplies most of the components that are necessary in order to run bytecode. This bytecode is normally much smaller than other programming languages in which executable programs are written through.

Basically, when used online, JAVA allows for applets to be used and downloaded through a browser. This allows the browser to access a feature or perform a function that would normally not be available without the applet. The program or applet must be downloaded or installed by the user before the user is able to fully access and use the JAVA program.

Chapter 2:
The Uses of JAVA

As of 2016, JAVA is utilized by over 9 million developers worldwide and is one of the most utilized programming languages available, especially for client-server applications. Regardless of a computer's architecture, the applications of JAVA are compiled to bytecode that runs on any JVM. JAVA used to be identified mainly with slow performance, waiting for drops from Sun Microsystems, bytecode interpretation, and the use of Applets. Today however, JAVA has become more associated with high performance, dynamic compilation of hotspots, a more and more independent open source community, and SOAs, web services, and web applications. This chapter will go into depth on the uses of the JAVA programming language, JAVA platforms, and the JAVA Virtual Machine.

Using JAVA Programming Language

The Java programming language is a high-level object-oriented programming language that is influenced in many different ways by Smalltalk, C, and C++ programming. The JAVA programming language has also borrowed some ideas from other languages. The syntactic design of JAVA programming language was made to be familiar to those already versed in "curly brace", C-descended languages, but has stronger (at times arguably) OO principles than the principles used in C++. The design of the JAVA programming language also incorporates a somewhat rigid system of exceptions which requires every method in the call stack to either declare its ability to throw exceptions or to declare its ability to handle them. Garbage collection is fairly automatic, or assumed, which does away with the need of the developer to have to free up memory used by objects that have become obsolete.

Java is philosophically referred to as a "fail early" language. Since it has syntax restrictions, most programming failures are just not actually possible with Java. Because JAVA has no direct access to pointers whatsoever, pointer-arithmetic errors simply don't exist. Utilizing an object as a different type than what it was originally named requires a straightforward cast conversion, which gives the compiler an obvious opportunity to deny programming that may be illogical.

Various Java enterprise frameworks necessitate the use of deployment descriptors or configuration files, which are usually written in XML, to identify a function. This could include the order of the steps that are needed to execute within a rule engine or which class may handle a particular request in HTTP. In other words, they must go beyond the language in order to implement their function. JAVA 5.0 adds footnotes to this language, and this allows for classes, fields, and methods to be tagged with values that then can be developed and inspected at runtime, and usually through reflection. Many programmers like these footnotes, usually referred to as annotations, because they simplify the things that may be otherwise addressed by certain deployment descriptors or some other means. They can also make it difficult to interpret the Java code, though. Whether or not a footnote or annotation is in place may affect the execution of the code, and may affect it in ways that may not be completely obvious from the footnote or annotation itself.

Aside from this singular criticism, JAVA is regarded as the most popular general-purpose computer programming language utilized at the present. JAVA programming is universally used as a standard in enterprise programming, and in 2005 replaced C++ as the programming language most widely utilized by Source Forge for its products. The benefits of JAVA programming language are extremely vast:

- An immense knowledge base.

- An enormous amount of developers that are readily available.

- Free tools which are available on numerous platforms such as Windows, Solaris, Linux and Mac. All of these platforms are able to execute and compile Java applications.

The Java programming language hits a unique and valuable point in the quid pro quo between code performance and developer efficiency. While CPU cycles continue to reduce in cost, developers usually do not. Because of this it may inevitably lead to the acceptance of another layer of abstraction between the execution of CPU opcodes and the developer – as long as it allows for the developer to create higher quality software at a much more efficient rate.

Using JAVA Platforms

Java is regarded generally in terms of three different platforms:

- The Enterprise Edition, also known as EE

- The Standard Edition, also known as SE

    And

- The Micro Edition, also known as ME

Each different platform describes the combination of a set of standard libraries, a language version, and a virtual machine to execute the code. EE is a superset of SE, meaning that any EE application can access and utilize the entirety of the SE libraries. Also, the EE's use of the programming language is identical to that of the SE's. This means that the SE is a subset of the EE.

Java Micro Edition is significantly different than its counterparts because of the fact that small devices (such as smart phones) are just simply much more limited on space and capabilities. The ME cannot be considered as a subset of the SE (therefore, cannot be considered a subset of the EE), because of the fact that a number of its libraries only exist in the Micro Edition. In addition, the ME version eliminates some programming language features because of the computation limitations of the platform on which it is run. Examples of some such eliminated features include Float class and the float primitive. This means that ME requires a different set of tools than EE and SE. With such deep seated differences in the devices that make the portability of code much less realistic in the micro space, a lot of Java developers view ME as a completely different animal altogether, almost a separate entity.

Using the JAVA Virtual Machine

JAVA source code has to translate into executable platform-native code at some point. Typically, this requires the use of a two-step process:

1. The developer needs to compile the source code into Java bytecode.

2. Then the Java Virtual Machine, JVM, translates this information to native code for the platform in use.

The second step was originally executed by interpretation, or taking each single JVM instruction and converting that instruction in an instant to one or more instructions native to the platform. After that is accomplished, the just-in-time compilers, referred to as JIT compilers, convert all of the Java program from JVM bytecode into platform-native code as the program is started up. There are several ways to achieve this conversion at this present time. Sun Microsystem's HotSpot compiler initializes this process by translating the code and profiling it at runtime, optimizing and compiling the particular areas that have been concluded to be the most critical to the program's successful operation. IBM's "mixed mode interpreter" of its JVMs works in a very similar fashion. These procedures circumvent the startup performance lag entailed by utilizing JIT compilers on the whole program, but this also means that performance is accumulated, arriving consistently over time, when critical code sections are detected and optimized. Because of this, client applications are less benefitted by this approach than the long-running server processes.

Using JAVA without JVM and Vice Versa

It is entirely possible to run Java without a JAVA Virtual Machine. Since Java source ends up becoming bytecode, then which in turn becomes platform-native code, as it stands, this can actually be accomplished all at one time. The GNU Compiler for JAVA, also referred to as GCJ, allows for an up front, one-time, compilation of JAVA source code into an executable command for a singular platform. Though there is enough information to compile command line and server side applications when using this process, it is not able to allow for the support of the Abstract Windowing Toolkit (AWT), which obviously renders it unsuitable for AWT programming and also Swing GUI programming.

The obvious downside to using this process is that cross-platform code ends up becoming bound to one single platform in one single step. What is more, the static compilation does not automatically trump the workings of HotSpot's dynamic compilation. The author of HotSpot's dynamic compilation once worked on a project in which the performance gain from GCJ was concluded to be less than five percent beyond the performance gain of the HotSpot version. Even still, GCJ does have the performance gain advantage and has the ability to solve crucial problems, such as the ability to deploy a particular Java application that is runnable without having to worry whether or not a JVM is currently running a specific version or whether or not JVM is currently available.

Using JVM without JAVA

It is also possible to get straight to the JVM level immediately and successfully bypass the Java language entirely. C-to-JVM bytecode compilers are already in existence; compilers like the Axiomatic Multi-Platform C, which is commercial and supplies a subset of ANSI C. What is more, the progress of Java bytecode manipulation using such tools as ASM and Apache BCEL, allow for the creation of classes at runtime that are completely executable in Java applications. This means that what you will be working with will no longer be Java, but instead will be an effective form of programming language used for assembly in the JVM.

Utilizing the JAVA Community Process

There is the Java community that exists beyond virtual machines, libraries, and programming language. In spite of the overwhelming amounts of open source software utilized by and written in Java, there is a continuously obvious and open conflict at large between the open source community and the Java community. This clash can be traced back mainly to Sun Microsystems' resistance in releasing its Java implementation under a fitting open-source license, even though this source is accessible under a plethora of Sun Microsystems-specified licenses.

Some people in these communities choose to state that this dissention is completely and ultimately misguided, at best. Bruno Souza, a developer, had this to say on the subject:

> "All of the Java standards that are there can be implemented completely as open source. This distinction between if the Java standard is run or not by an organization outside of Sun, I don't think that matters that much. The most important thing is that the rules of the JCP are very clear ... The JCP is a very open standards organization. Of course, it's not perfect. But I think that one very important thing is that the standards the JCP generates, you can implement open source implementations of the Java standards. And that's extremely important, because that's the combination we want...."

"You say Java's not open source ... that's a totally meaningless statement. Because it means nothing to say that Java is or isn't open source. It's like saying HTTP is or isn't open source; it doesn't mean anything."

The JAVA Community Process, sometimes referred to as simply the JCP, was established in 1998. The JCP is the formalized mechanism by which any interested parties may be allowed to offer input in the development of standard technical specs of the JAVA technology. It is open to the public and anyone may become a member of the JAVA Community Process by simply submitting the appropriate form available at their website.

Beyond the JAVA Community Process

A hugely wide range of Java projects exist entirely outside of the standardized acceptations of the JCP. As noted previously, Java is the programming language used the most, by far, for projects on SourceForge, and even more open source Java projects are able to be accessed at the Apache Jakarta Project, java.net, Javaforge (of Javalobby), OpenSymphony, and an immeasurable amount of other independent websites. A lot of these independent projects have grown enough to actually rival the official JCP standards in the level of awareness in the minds of JCP consumers. As a whole, these independent projects have also been able to be quick to adapt to modifications completely outside of Java and also simultaneously utilize their best features, such as the AJAX-simplifying Direct Web Remoting (DWR) project or the Rails-inspired Trails project.

Chapter 3:
JAVA Basics

When it comes to learning JAVA programming language, or any programming language for that matter, there are five basic concepts you must understand before you get started. These five basic concepts include:

1. Variables

2. Data Structures

3. Control Structures

4. Syntax

5. Tools

Each of these concepts will be thoroughly explained on a beginner's level to ensure that they are understood.

Variables

Variables are the cornerstone of any and all JAVA programs you will encounter, and as such they are the cornerstone of JAVA programming language. By definition, a variable in computer programming is simply the location of storage as well as the associated name that symbolizes what an unknown or known information or quantity may be. In other words, a particular value. Simply put, a variable is a method of storing some kind of information for use at a later time, and is retrievable by referring to a name or word which will describe said information.

For example, if you to a certain website, the very first thing this website does is ask you what your name is. This is normally done in order to instate some form of human familiarity – upon your next visit, that website will call you by name. The person who built the website would create a small text box on the screen that would ask you for your name and that small text box would represent a variable. The person who built the page may decide to call that small text box something like "Visitor Name", and that would be the symbolic word or name for the small text box variable.

So then, after you type your name into the small text box, your name is stored as information in a variable called "Visitor Name". This information would be made available to the person who built the page, or the programmer. This person would then be able to come back and ask "What value does the variable "Visitor Name" contain?", and the program would answer the programmer with the value of whatever you may have typed into that small text box that you saw when you first visited the page.

This concept is used constantly throughout programming and is also super powerful in programming. This concept makes Twitter and Facebook work; it is what allows you to pay your bills using your online bank, and it is also what makes it possible to place a bid on sites like eBay. Variables enable the programming world to keep spinning 'round, as it were.

Okay, now it is time to get a bit more specific. There are different types of variables when it comes to programming using the Java programming language. If a programmer were to store your name in a variable, your name would be stored as a type of variable called a *String*. Or, perhaps the programmer also wanted to store your age - that would be stored as a type of variable known as an *Integer*. Finally, maybe the programmer wanted to store your yearly income – your income would then be stored as a type of variable referred to as a *Double*. Just to recap, there are three different types of variables being covered here:

- String

- Integer

- Double

So, what exactly constitutes a String, an Integer and a Double? With Java, the programming language needs to know what sort of information you will be going to store within a particular variable. The programming language needs to know this because Java is what is known as a strongly typed language. Basically, in order for a language to be weakly typed, that means that the types of all of the variables are inferred, or known at the time of compilation. A strongly typed language, however, does not allow for the use of one type as another type, meaning that it utilizes different types of variables. This is where string, integer, and double variables are put to use.

String

Typing in Java lets the programming language know 100% that the information being stored within a variable will be concretely defined. When a string is referred to in JAVA, we are looking at the data as if it were simply a sentence in the English language. A String just specifically represents letters placed in a specific order. As in the English language, string variables constitute a series of letters placed in a particular order which gives that series of letters meaning.

In the way that string variables are made more understandable by comparing it to everyday language, adding two strings together works very much the same way.

If you have two sting variables and they stored, for example, the data "Visitor" and "Name", if they were added together you would get the String: "VisitorName".

Integer

In Java, an integer variable means you have a number that does not include decimal places. This means a whole number such as 23 or -784. In Java, when it is specified that a variable is an integer, it is simply not allowable to store anything but a whole number.

For example, if you want to add two numbers together, the number 25 and the number 2. Java will behave differently depending on the type of the variable that's storing this data. Then adding 25 and 2 together will result in the integer 27. Instead of just compounding the two, as a string would, the integers are added together using simple math.

Double

The double variable in JAVA can either hold very large or very small numbers. The minimum and maximum values are respectively both 17 followed by 307 zeros.

The double variable is also used to hold floating point values. A floating point value is basically any numerical value with a decimal point.

The bottom line is, having a type will help you start to understand what sort of things you are able to do with the information contained within the variable. Types of variables are really powerful and make sense of what is and what is not allowed within a certain variable group.

Data Structures

A data structure in computer science is a specific method of organizing and storing information in a computer so that it may be used in an efficient manner. To better explain data structures, let's use the concept of a list of contacts. Usually, a list of contacts contains numerous contacts which could shrink or grow at any time. For this example, let's say you need to keep five contacts in order. If you were to attempt to represent those contacts as variables in a program, you would need to know data structure.

In this instance, you have a list of contacts. With Java, there is a data structure called a list. This is what the code looks like:

1. List contacts = new ArrayList();

Do not worry about the symbols yet, that will be covered later. All you need to know at the moment is that there is a way to store a list into a data structure. In a List data structure you can easily both add and remove items from your list.

contacts.add("John Doe (john.doe@somename.com)");

contacts.add("Jane Doe (jane.doe@somename.com)");

When creating a data structure, it is supremely more efficient to create one variable, as shown above, instead of a different variable that you would need to write out for every single item on your list. Because you only created one variable, contacts.add(RandomContact) that means that your code is more dynamic and flexible. In this instance, dynamic refers to the fact that the outcome of the program is able to change depending on which variables are inputted. You ideally want your code to be rendered as dynamic as possible, and you want it to have the ability to handle a lot of situations without needing to keep writing more and more code as time goes on. Basically, data structure is just a way to avoid having to create more variables than necessary.

Control Structures

A control structure is a block of programming that analyzes variables and chooses a flow based on given parameters. It is the basic process where decisions are made in computing. Flow control regulates how a computer responds when given specific conditions and parameters. This means that while a program is running, the code is read by the computer line by line. This process is known as "code flow". As the code is read from top to bottom, it may reach a point that requires decision-making. This decision could result in the code jumping to a different part of that program, it may require that a piece is rerun, or it may skip a lot of code in response. This process could be equated to a choose-your-own-adventure book. You reach page 12 of the book, and you have a choice between selection A and selection B. A computer program works much the same way except the program has a strict set of rules to abide by. The decision that the program makes effects the flow of code, and that is known as a control structure.

Syntax

The syntax of a programming language is really the set of rules which define the combinations of symbols considered to be precisely structured programs in that set language. Syntax is basically a particular layout of symbols. In JAVA, an example of this would be curly brackets {} or round brackets (). For example, when you look at an email address you are able to identify the fact that it is an email address. You are able to recognize an email address and differentiate it from a website address because of the different syntax contained therein. Syntax in JAVA programming language is similar. There are rules in place, and when followed, allows programming language to comprehend and create functioning software. You will receive errors if you do not abide by the rules of a programming languages' syntax.

In JAVA, there are four steps to the syntax of creating a variable:

1. The first part is the word String, which is the variable's type. A String in this particular case allows the storage of regular letters as well as special characters.

2. The second part is the variable name. A variable name can be made up of numbers and letters, but the only special characters they are allowed are underscores. Variable names normally start with a lower case letter. This is not a must, but is kind of a rule of thumb in the JAVA world.

3. The third part is the value that the particular variable holds. In JAVA, strings are defined by placing quotes around regular numbers, letters, and special characters.

4. The fourth and final part is the mark of completion. In Java, a semi-colon is used. Although there are some exceptions, nearly all lines of JAVA code end in a semi-colon, much like a period at the end of a sentence.

Tools

A tool used in programming is much like any other tool in that it helps you to accomplish your goal more efficiently. In JAVA, a tool is a piece of software that enables you to get your program completed more quickly. There is a vast array of tools used in JAVA programming, but for all intents and purposes, this book will focus on the IDE.

An Integrated Development Environment, or IDE is software that will make coding a lot easier. IDEs check the syntax of code to make sure there are no errors. IDEs also organize your files and give you a specific way to view them. IDEs tend to incorporate code completion, which actually fills in code for you, in some common scenarios. IDEs enable easy navigation through code. There are many more advantages of using an IDE, though the most useful are noted here.

Chapter 4:
JAVA Commands

There are way too many JAVA commands to list here, but this book includes some of the most common and useful commands available. They are in no particular order, except for the first being a very common starting point for newbie programmers.

Hello World

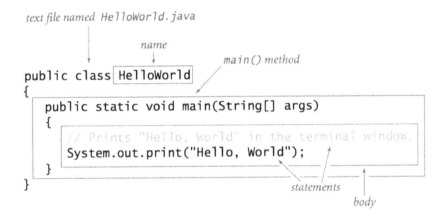

Integers

values			integers between -2^{31} and $+2^{31}-1$			
typical literals			1234 99 0 1000000			
operations	sign	add	subtract	multiply	divide	remainder
operators	+ -	+	-	*	/	%

expression	value	comment
99	99	integer literal
+99	99	positive sign
-99	-99	negative sign
5 + 3	8	addition
5 - 3	2	subtraction
5 * 3	15	multiplication
5 / 3	1	no fractional part
5 % 3	2	remainder
1 / 0		run-time error
3 * 5 - 2	13	* has precedence
3 + 5 / 2	5	/ has precedence
3 - 5 - 2	-4	left associative
(3 - 5) - 2	-4	better style
3 - (5 - 2)	0	unambiguous

Using an Object

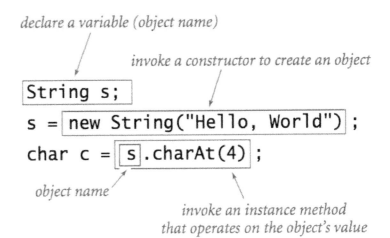

declare a variable (object name)

invoke a constructor to create an object

```
String s;
s = new String("Hello, World") ;
char c = s.charAt(4) ;
```

object name

invoke an instance method
that operates on the object's value

Classes

class name

instance variables

constructor

instance variable names

instance methods

test client

create and initialize object

invoke constructor

object name

invoke method

```java
public class Charge
{
   private final double rx, ry;
   private final double q;

   public Charge(double x0, double y0, double q0)
   {   rx = x0; ry = y0; q = q0;   }

   public double potentialAt(double x, double y)
   {
      double k = 8.99e09;
      double dx = x - rx;
      double dy = y - ry;
      return k * q / Math.sqrt(dx*dx + dy*dy);
   }

   public String toString()
   {   return q +" at " + "("+ rx + ", " + ry +")";   }

   public static void main(String[] args)
   {
      double x = Double.parseDouble(args[0]);
      double y = Double.parseDouble(args[1]);
      Charge c1 = new Charge(0.51, 0.63, 21.3);
      Charge c2 = new Charge(0.13, 0.94, 81.9);
      double v1 = c1.potentialAt(x, y);
      double v2 = c2.potentialAt(x, y);
      StdOut.printf("%.2e\n", (v1 + v2));
   }
}
```

JAVA's String Data Type

```
public class String
```

	String(String s)	*create a string with the same value as* s
int	length()	*number of characters*
char	charAt(int i)	*the character at index* i
String	substring(int i, int j)	*characters at indices* i *through* (j-1)
boolean	contains(String substring)	*does this string contain* substring?
boolean	startsWith(String pre)	*does this string start with* pre?
boolean	endsWith(String post)	*does this string end with* post?
int	indexOf(String pattern)	*index of first occurrence of* pattern
int	indexOf(String pattern, int i)	*index of first occurrence of* pattern *after* i
String	concat(String t)	*this string with* t *appended*
int	compareTo(String t)	*string comparison*
String	toLowerCase()	*this string, with lowercase letters*
String	toUpperCase()	*this string, with uppercase letters*
String	replaceAll(String a, String b)	*this string, with* as *replaced by* bs
String[]	split(String delimiter)	*strings between occurrences of* delimiter
boolean	equals(Object t)	*is this string's value the same as* t's?
int	hashCode()	*an integer hash code*

Anatomy of an "If" Statement

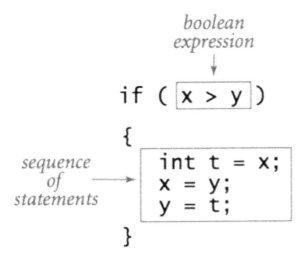

If and If-else Statements

absolute value	`if (x < 0) x = -x;`
| *put the smaller value in x and the larger value in y* | ```
if (x > y)
{
    int t = x;
    x = y;
    y = t;
}
``` |
| *maximum of x and y* | ```
if (x > y) max = x;
else       max = y;
``` |
| *error check for division operation* | ```
if (den == 0) System.out.println("Division by zero");
else          System.out.println("Quotient = " + num/den);
``` |
| *error check for quadratic formula* | ```
double discriminant = b*b - 4.0*c;
if (discriminant < 0.0)
{
    System.out.println("No real roots");
}
else
{
    System.out.println((-b + Math.sqrt(discriminant))/2.0);
    System.out.println((-b - Math.sqrt(discriminant))/2.0);
}
``` |

Anatomy of a Loop

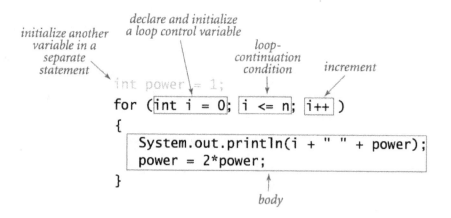

initialize another variable in a separate statement

declare and initialize a loop control variable

loop-continuation condition

increment

```
int power = 1;
for (int i = 0; i <= n; i++ )
{
    System.out.println(i + " " + power);
    power = 2*power;
}
```

body

Loops

compute the largest power of 2 less than or equal to n	```int power = 1;
while (power <= n/2)
power = 2*power;
System.out.println(power);```
compute a finite sum ($1 + 2 + ... + n$)	```int sum = 0;
for (int i = 1; i <= n; i++)
sum += i;
System.out.println(sum);```
compute a finite product ($n! = 1 \times 2 \times ... \times n$)	```int product = 1;
for (int i = 1; i <= n; i++)
product *= i;
System.out.println(product);```
print a table of function values	```for (int i = 0; i <= n; i++)
System.out.println(i + " " + 2*Math.PI*i/n);```
compute the ruler function (see PROGRAM 1.2.1)	```String ruler = "1";
for (int i = 2; i <= n; i++)
ruler = ruler + " " + i + " " + ruler;
System.out.println(ruler);```

Chapter 5:
Learning JAVA Step by Step

1. **Install JAVA JDK.**

    -   Open your browser and search for JAVA JDK

    -   Look for an option from Oracle.com and click

    -   Click on the JAVA JDK download

    -   Click to accept license

    -   Choose your operating system

    -   Minimize everything else on your computer

    -   Once it is downloaded, be ready to run the executable file

    -   Click next and check status

    -   JAVA JDK will start installing

    -   Click next and wait for JAVA to finish installing

    -   Once installed, you can go to your C folder and you should see two files, JDK and JRE

2. **Install and set up Eclipse IDE**

    -   Go to www.eclipse.org

    -   Download eclipse IDE for JAVA developers

    -   Choose your operating system

- You will then be directed to choose your PC's nearest location, so click the location that is nearest to you

- You will then be prompted to save the zip file, save zip file

- Open the zip file once it is finished downloading

- Minimize everything else on your computer

- The zip file contains a folder named eclipse, extract to C folder

- Once the extraction is complete, you should be able to see eclipse in your C folder

- Open eclipse

- The first time you open eclipse, you will be asked where you want your projects to be saved, choose a location or leave it at C folder default

- Click OK and eclipse should open shortly

- To create a new project go to file, then new, then JAVA project

- Name your project

- Capitalize the first letter of each word in your project name

- Click next

- Click finish

- Your "My Project" folder is created

3. Create your first JAVA project in Eclipse IDE

- Create a new JAVA project in eclipse

- You will see that eclipse will also create a subdirectory for the project you create, this will contain your source file

- Close all projects except for the project you will be working on

- Right click on the source folder of the project you want to work on and you will be able to add packages to your folder (whenever you add a package it will add a folder to your source folder)

- Access the package you just created and you will be able to create a new class

- When naming your class, make sure the first letter of each word of the name you choose is capitalized

- You will be asked which method stop you would like to create, check public static void mean

- Press finish

- You will want to include a comment section in your project; in order to do this you will first start with a forward slash, followed by an asterisk, then press enter

- This comment section is not executed by your program, it is only info you are documenting for your program

- Another way of creating comments is by first starting with two forward slashes and posting your comment after; this will not be executed either

- Whatever you write in the main class will be executed

- JAVA has built-in classes to help you program; the most important of these is called System – make sure the S is capitalized

- When you type System then a period eclipse will automatically know what to do; it should look like this: System.

- A popup menu will then appear, showing you the available methods of a label in this system class

- Select the method called out.println

- Once that is selected, you will then be able to click on it and start leaving a comment

- When you are ready to run your program, right click on your project and run as JAVA application – or – you can click the "run my class" option, which will open the save and launch popup

- Whenever you scroll over a built-in method of class in eclipse editor it will give you a help popup which shows you what that particular code can be used for

4. Variables and Types in JAVA

- When declaring a variable in JAVA you must first select the data type

- For example, let's say you want to store an integer in a variable

- Declare the data type as "int" (for integer)

- Name your variable, say you name your variable x

- Assign value to your variable, such as 10

- Your line of code should now look like this: int x = 10;

- You can also directly use your variable in the System.out.println line

- Instead of typing a message in this line, you can put x as the value; your line should then look like this: System.out.println(x);

- When you run this program, the value you assigned to x, which is 10, will be printed where the x is in the line

- Basic data types include

    a. byte (number, 1 byte)

    b. short (number, 2 bytes)

    c. int (number, 4 bytes)

    d. long (number, 8 bytes)

    e. float (float number, 4 bytes)

    f. double (float number, 8 bytes)

    g. char (a character, 2 bytes)

h. boolean (true or false, 1 byte)

- Byte, short, int, and long can all store a number, the only difference is their size – as indicated in parentheses

- The range of all of the variables increases with byte size

- Short example: short my_variable=10;

- When using the float variable, you need to include the word float into your code: float my_decimal=(float)4.5;

- When using the double variable, it is not necessary to differentiate and should look like this: double my_double=11.52;

- Use char if you want to store any one single character: char my_char='A';

- Boolean can store true or false: boolean is_true=false;

- When printed out, only the values of all of these variables would appear, so in order they would show up as 10, 4.5, 11.52, A, and false

5. Getting user input using JAVA

- There is a class in JAVA called Scanner which enables you receive input and looks like this: Scanner scan=new Scanner(System.in);

- In order to be able to give output in the same line, it should look like this: Scanner scan=new Scanner(System.out);

- If you want to gather input from a user, your first line of code should be: System.out.println("Enter some number");

- you then want to name your variable and continue coding:

  int user_input_number = scan.

- When you reach the part in the second line at scan., eclipse will then prompt you to make a choice, here you want to choose next int, so the completed second line will look like this: int user_input_number = scan.next int();

- Now if you want to print this value, that line of code should look like this: System.out.println("The entered value is");

- If you want to print your output without breaking the line, first omit the ln after print in the line code, then copy your variable, which in this case is user_input_number, then paste it in the parentheses and run your program, the last line should look like this: System.out.print(user_input_number);

- When you've run this program, you will notice that it asks the user to enter a value. Let's say you enter the value of 1,000

- Once you enter the value, the program will confirm the entered value

- Double works the same way, but you have to make sure you are consistent in changing the entire line of code, for example:

```
Scanner scan1 = new Scanner (System.in);

System.out.println("Enter some decimal value");

double user_input_double = scan1.nextdouble();

System.out.println("The entered value is");

System.out.print(user_input_double);
```

- If you want to take text input, you need to define the variable as string

- Take the previous code and just change it scan.next line, because you are expecting a line from the user

- The entire program should then look like this:

```
Scanner scan1 = new Scanner (System.in);

System.out.println("Enter some string");

string user_input_string = scan1.nextLine();

System.out.println("The entered string is");

System.out.print(user_input_string);
```

- When you run this program you will be prompted to enter some string, enter a phrase of your choosing

6. Math and arithmetic operators in JAVA

- First, declare two variables, x and y in this instance

- Then assign an answer

- int x, y, answer;

- Assign value to x and y, 20 and 30 respectively

- Assign value to the answer, 50

- If you want to print out your answer, the program should look like this:

      int x, y, answer;

      x = 20;

      y = 30;

      answer = x + y;

      System.out.println("Answer = " + answer);

- When an addition or plus symbol is used in a print function, it is known as a *concatenation* or *concatenation operator*

- The correct answer should be printed out in eclipse without you actually having to do the math, as long as the code is correct

- In order to perform a subtraction, all you need to do is replace the addition symbol with the subtraction symbol in the fourth line of code, or the answer line: answer = x − y;

- When performing multiplication, x cannot be used as the multiplication symbol because x is often a variable; instead, an asterisk is used

- All you have to do to perform multiplication is replace the symbol again: answer = x * y;

- Division is a little bit trickier – if you divide a lower number by a higher number and have declared your variable as integer, the answer will always be zero because integers cannot be decimals

- In the same light, when your variable has been declared as integer and you are dividing a higher number that is not divisible by a lower number without using decimals, you will not get an exactly mathematically correct answer either – if you try to divide seventy by thirty, your answer will be two because that is how many times thirty can go into seventy while having a whole number as an answer

- In order to get accurate answers in division, you must declare your variables as double

- A forward slash symbol is used in place of the other symbols when using division

- One more operator in JAVA is called the modulus operator and it gives you the remainder of a division

7. Increment operator and assignment operator

- An increment operator is used when you would like to increase the value of a variable and somewhat resembles algebra

- int x = 10;

    x = x + 1;

    System.out.println(x);

- Another way of writing this code to achieve the same goal would be to replace the + 1 with two addition symbols, this is called post increment operation

- int x = 10;

    x++;

    System.out.println(x);

- The same answer of eleven has been reached both times in print

- If you use x++ in the print line it looks like this:

    int x = 10;

    System.out.println(x++);

- In post increment operation , the value of x will only be changed after this plus plus operation

- Now you are going to increase the value of x by one which should look like this:

    int x = 10;

    System.out.println(x++);

    System.out.println(x);

- Pre increment operation places the plus symbols in front of the x and increases its value before the operation is performed

- So if we add ++x in place of x++ in the previous code, this is what you would see:

  int x = 10;

  System.out.println(++x);

  System.out.println(x);

- The answer to this is actually

  11

  11

  This is because the pre increment operator, where x had a value of 11 and the post increment operator, where x also had a value of 11 were compiled

- Now let's say you want to add five to this value, you can do it by writing out: x = x + 5

- Another way of writing this is: x+ = 5

- If you would like to multiply the value of 5 and the value of 10 in the equation, you would only need to replace the addition symbol in x+ =5 with an asterisk – that shortcut works for multiplication as well – and it would look like this: x* = 5

- The term 'equal to' in JAVA is referred to as assignment operator

- Thus, x* = 5 and x = x*5 is an assignment operator and this operator works for addition, subtraction, multiplication and division

8. If else or conditional statements and relational operators

- A conditional statement is a statement which evaluates whether a condition is true or false, and based upon this condition executes a certain code

- A double equal sign == symbolizes relational operator

- An if statement looks like this:

    int x = 10;

    if (x == 10) {

    System.out.println("yes x == 10");

    This statement is basically saying if x is equal to 10, then I want to run this code. Here, the program answers that yes, x is in fact equal to 10, which is true

- That means the statement is followed and the condition will be executed

- Now try to see if x is equal to 20 by only changing the statement by placing the number 20 in the if line

- No answer will come up in eclipse because this statement is false and the condition cannot be executed

- An if else statement can execute when an if statement does not and looks like this:

    int x = 10;

    if (x == 20) {

        System.out.println("yes x == 10");

    }

    else {

        System.out.println("no x != 10");

- Take note of the exclamation point that has taken the place of one of the equal signs after the else line – this is called a non-equality operator

- Now when you run the program again eclipse will give you the answer that x is in fact not equal to 10

- In JAVA, comparison operators include

    a. == is equal to

    b. != is not equal to

    c. >   is greater than

    d. <   is less than

    e. >= is greater than or equal to

    f. <= is less than or equal to

9. Logical operators in JAVA

- If you want to evaluate more than one condition using a simple if statement or an if else statement you will need to use a logical operator

- There are two basic kinds of logical operators – the and operator, which is symbolized by double ampersands && and the second type is called an or operator which is symbolized by double pipe symbols ||

- The and operator and the or operator can both be used to define two conditions simultaneously in both if and if else statements

- The and operator checks to see if all conditions are simultaneously true while the or operator checks to see if one or more things is true

- The symbol placed between subjects tells which you are using, as in line four of the following two codes

  int subject1 = 40;

  int subject2 = 60;

  // && ->AND || ->OR

  if ((subject1 >= 35) && (subject2 >= 35)) {

    System.out.println("the condition is true");

  This condition is true because both 40 and 60 are greater than 35

- Now try to incorporate an else statement with the if statement, nut first change the value of subject1 to 20

if else

int subject1 = 20;

int subject2 = 60;

// && ->AND || ->OR

if ((subject1 >= 35) && (subject2 >= 35)) {

   System.out.println("the condition is true");

} else {

   System.out.println("the condition is false");

This condition is false

- Now try running the same program but replace the and operator with the or operator:

int subject1 = 40;

int subject2 = 60;

// && ->AND || ->OR

if ((subject1 >= 35) || (subject2 >= 35)) {

   System.out.println("the condition is true");

} else {

   System.out.println("the condition is false");

This condition is true

10. Switch statement in JAVA

- Whenever you have to check multiple in JAVA, you will want to utilize the conditions switch statement

  - You can also switch statements in place of if else statements

  - The breaks in a switch statement act to break up the responses you will receive from the programwhen you run it

- Part of a switch statement includes the use of 'default' which works like the else in an if else statement

- int = 90;

// byte, int, short, or char.

switch (score)

{

case 90 :

System.out.println("Very good");

break;

case 60 :

System.out.println("Good");

break;

case 30 :

System.out.println("OK");

break;

default :

System.out.println("Grades are not defined");

break;

}

With the value of the integer identified as 90, the case 90 statement is true.

- When there is no break between case statements, the program will default to the next lowest in succession when utilizing this type of code

11. The while statements, or while loops

- While loops are the most basic loops in JAVA

- A loop is a piece of code or a statement which executes some block of code again and again until some condition is met

- If you want to execute some code again and again without having to rewrite it over and over, this is what loop is for:

```
int a = 0;

while (a <=10)

{
```

```
System.out.println(a);

a++;

}
```

12. Do while statements, or do while loops

- The basic difference between a while loop and a do while loop is that while loops first evaluate the condition and then execute the code, whereas do while loops execute the code first and then evaluate the condition

13. Arrays in JAVA

- An array is similar to a variable but it can store more than one value at a time – the only condition being that even though you can store more than one value in an array, it has to be the same type of values

- For example, you would be able to store 10 integers in an array, but if you wanted to store 5 integers and 5 doubles, you would not be able to do it

- This is one way of declaring an array: int [] myintarray = {4, 2,1,5,3};

- Another way is: int myinarray2[] = {4,2,1,5,3} This way is fine but it is not the preferred way of declaring an array

- There are three more ways of declaring arrays

    1. int[] myIntArray = new int[3];

    2. int[] myIntArray = {1,2,3};

3. int[] myIntArray = new int []{1,2,3};

14. JAVA string

- A string is a sequence of characters and can also be known as an array of characters

- In order declare a string in JAVA, you just use the keyword 'string'

- You then name your string whatever you would like

- Then you place an equal sign after that

- Then in double quotes, place whatever string you want to assign and print it just the same as all the others:

  String mystring = "Hello World";

  System.out.println(mystring)

15. Introduction to methods

- The terms method and function can be used somewhat interchangeably, but the preferred term in JAVA is method

- A method is a piece of code which executes some logic and you can wrap this method with a name and you can recall this method as many times as you would like whenever you want to use it

- You can name your method anything you wish

- This is the most basic kind of method:

```java
public static void myFirstMethod() {

}
```

- The term 'public static' is known as the pacifier

- If you want to print a message using method, this is what the syntax or code would look like:

```java
public static void myFirstMethod() {

    System.out.println("Hello Youtube");

}
```

Conclusion

Thanks again for taking the time to read this book!

You should now have a good understanding of JAVA Programming and be able to do some basic JAVA Programming!

If you enjoyed this book, please take the time to leave me a review on Amazon. I appreciate your honest feedback, and it really helps me to continue producing high quality books.